Santa Fe Modern

Contemporary Design in the High Desert

Santa Fe

Helen Thompson

Foreword by Laura Carpenter

Photographs by Casey Dunn

 Modern

Contents

Foreword

Laura Carpenter

In 1974, as a twenty-five-year-old contemporary art dealer in Dallas, Texas, I came to Santa Fe to scope out its art community. One of the first people I met was the abstract landscape painter Forrest Moses, who invited me to his house. Standing in his home/studio, I noted the diverse mix of adobe architecture, modern furniture, objects, and art, and I was smitten. Forrest's realm was an exquisite combination of American Indian, Asian, flea market, modern, and contemporary styles. I knew then that Santa Fe was where I wanted to live and work.

To observe the evolving Santa Fe style—the way old and new, smooth and rough, indoor and outdoor, high design and junkyard, sophisticated and mundane mixed—was liberating. I loved it all, for quirky reasons. Adobe walls seemed so authentic compared to the stark utilitarian Sheetrock I was used to seeing in Dallas houses. And I loved the kind of temperature control here—open windows in the summer and radiant heat in the winter. No mosquitoes or flies here either, and that made me very happy. Sitting outside on a summer night is one of my biggest pleasures—just the feeling of the air is wonderful, plus the sky and vistas can be grand while adjacent intimate courtyards are full of surprises. Santa Fe is a real desert oasis with the added attraction of diversely eccentric residents, and it became my home.

I rented a house in 1974 and came here as often as I could. I finally made the permanent move to Santa Fe in 1989 and established Laura Carpenter Fine Art. The idea of opening an art gallery specializing in cutting-edge art may seem counterintuitive, but I had done my research and felt that it would work. Many visitors come for the art and enjoy seeing it in a gallery setting.

We opened in a landmarked 1879 adobe building across the river from downtown but still within walking distance. The pitched-roof structure had high ceilings, nicely proportioned rooms, and thick walls. I relished the idea of exhibiting contemporary paintings, drawings, and sculpture in that historic building as opposed to displaying them in sterile, hard-edged spaces with the dreaded white Sheetrock walls.

The building had always been a mustard yellow color with white trim. That color had been its identity for decades, but when I began remodeling, it caught the attention of the Historic Districts Review Board whose job it is to keep the Santa Fe look intact. For the Downtown and Eastside districts, the ordinance recognizes two principal styles—Old Santa Fe (defined as Spanish-Pueblo or Territorial) and New Santa Fe, more contemporary architecture that complements the materials, color, proportion, and overall detail of the old style. The review board wanted the building painted brown to conform with its rules, but I argued that the color preceded their rules, established in 1957. I won the battle, and it was determined that the house would remain yellow. It was a rare exception to the zoning ordinances, which was probably philosophically appropriate for my new gallery. I expected that some of the art I would show would challenge rules, too.

The gallery began showing contemporary artists with international reputations: Richard Tuttle, Louise Bourgeois, Ellsworth Kelly, Marina Abramović, and James Lee Byars. Dwight Hackett opened the Art Foundry, which not only collaborated with artists but also challenged the limits of traditional casting techniques and drew sculptors like Kiki Smith, Juan Muñoz, Bruce Nauman, Tristano di Robilant, and Terry Allen into its orbit. Although several of these artists lived in the Santa Fe area and were already famous, they were just beginning to be recognized locally.

Going to galleries became an activity that brought people to Santa Fe—it was something they expected to do. And they knew that we would have something or someone provocative, such as the Serbian performance artist, writer, filmmaker, and philanthropist Marina Abramović. Her work explores body art, endurance art, and feminist art, and especially the relationship between the performer and audience. When we staged an exhibition of her work, she did not disappoint. At the opening, one of the two rooms at the gallery's entry was empty except for a chair in the center of the space and the floor, which was covered with dry ice (there was plastic sheeting under the ice). Mid-opening, a robed Marina was escorted to the chair by one of my staff members, a gentleman from Mexico who was not yet that familiar with contemporary art or art openings. To his shock and pretty much everyone else's, Marina dropped her robe and seated herself nude on the chair. The staff then brought in pythons and draped them over Marina where she sat for the rest of the opening, the dry ice on the floor diverting the snakes from everyone except Marina whose body warmth drew them to her. The most astounding thing for me was that Marina did not know the snakes; they were "rentals" from local snake owners that we found in town. Marina said she had grown up afraid of snakes, and this was her way of combating that fear.

James Lee Byars lived in Santa Fe when I had the gallery. Byars was an American conceptual and performance artist who also considered himself a mystic. He was also something of a dandy, incorporating his personal esoteric motifs into his daily dress. For his exhibition, James Lee insisted that the gallery walls be gold-leafed and that Whitney Houston be invited to give a concert from the gallery parking lot. James Lee's work (and James Lee himself) was very theatrical, and he wanted the setting to reflect that theatricality. Suffice to say, these requests were not granted, but I did surprise him by covering the gallery walls with plywood and painting them gold, which seemed to please him.

That exhibit encouraged some of us like-minded contemporary art collectors to do more, and so by 1992 we came up the idea of a consortium that would fund a nonprofit facility to mount temporary exhibitions. I was able to raise more than $1 million for the project, a third of which went to New York architect Richard Gluckman who designed a renovation of a warehouse near the Railyard into 19,000 square feet of exhibition space. SITE Santa Fe, as we named it, initiated a local, contemporary focus on modern design and was, at the time, the only international biennial of contemporary art in the United States. SITE officially opened in 1995—for the biennial's first edition, curator Bruce Ferguson and co-curator Vince Varga selected thirty-one artists—half of them women—from thirteen different countries to participate.

The contemporary art space now draws global attention with its yearly exhibitions. Richard Gluckman went on to design the Georgia O'Keeffe Museum, and SITE Santa Fe now has a handsome new building by the innovative SHoP Architects. Since its founding, SITE Santa Fe has presented eleven biennials, more than ninety contemporary art exhibitions, and works by more than eight hundred artists. Following the success of the first international biennial of contemporary art in the United States, SITE expanded its programming to include ongoing exhibitions of notable artists, as well as new commissions and U.S. debuts. SITE also supports New Mexico-based artists with career development opportunities and maintains active outreach such as public and educational programs related to each exhibition, conversations with artists and curators, film screenings, performances, concerts, workshops, and collaborations with Santa Fe public schools.

The Railyard area where SITE Santa Fe is located has become a second plaza for the city, a vibrant place that centers on art. The original plaza still thrives, a first destination for visitors to the city, but Santa Fe has been deliberate in maintaining its aesthetic integrity, even in parts of the city that depend on tourists. That is one of the reasons I have stayed here. The weather, the architecture, the lifestyle are irresistible—and I still find the spirit of the city just as liberating now as I did when I was in my twenties. But maybe it's even simpler than that. Santa Fe is a place where I can sit outside at night, where it's possible for me to look into the dark night sky and give my ideas free rein and from there to think my best thoughts.

Introduction

Santa Fe might be the only city in the United States best approached by car. I have made the 54-mile journey on I-25 many times, the mundane four-lane highway heading away from Albuquerque's barren terrain into something else quite magical. With each mile comes a frisson of separation, detaching me from the twenty-first century and edging toward something visibly retrograde and, to my mind, far preferable. The cadence of geological time is hard to ignore, exposed and harsh and free of thoughtless clutter like signage. This is an immense basin, its size the endgame of eons of geological upheaval, and a resolute reminder that here in the high desert even the most casual observer must adopt a long-range perspective.

And so, as Santa Fe comes into view across a vast and high plain embraced by the Jemez and the Sangre de Cristo Mountains, the city of 85,000 unobtrusively emerges from the foothills of the surrounding mountains. The setting is colossal, and the low brown adobe buildings of suburbs and town respect the view. They are the color of the earth and appear to have always been there, which is almost the truth.

The past is supreme in New Mexico. It defines everything, even modern architecture, which has become relevant here in recent decades. Modernism has its antecedents in pre-Columbian building traditions that thrived in a 130,000-square-mile swath of the American Southwest. Efficient and—in hindsight—elegant, these square or rectangular volumes were plainly fundamental, built of earthy materials such as mud and straw or stone. Sometimes they were carved into canyon walls. The cube-like structures radiate unity—linked either by a minimalist anatomy or arranged in clusters—evoking domesticity, community, and a reverence for the environment, both earthly and celestial. Their purpose was straightforward: to house, to connect, and to protect.

I'm using the term "past" to refer to the distant reaches of time from about 900 to 1350 CE when the Ancestral Puebloan culture prospered. Hundreds of communities in Colorado, New Mexico, Utah, Nevada, and Arizona comprised a complex network that was connected by a system of roads and way stations. The stone dwellings still exist and are part of the largest collection of indigenous architecture in the United States. Now protected inside national parks, these dwellings can be found in the Chaco Culture National Historical Park, Mesa Verde National Park, Bandelier National Monument, Hovenweep National Monument, and Canyon de Chelly National Monument. But it's not just the buildings that link us to the past: Pueblo tribes—Zuni, Acoma, Hopi, and Laguna—still thrive and they trace their lineage to the Ancestral Puebloans.

The Puebloans' guileless, pragmatic building style is the unlikely philosophical precursor in this part of the world to the modernist movement. Both embraced functionality and rejected decoration. But the ancient architecture was also a casualty, its mien too unassuming to withstand the onslaught of statement-making building traditions of Greco-Roman cultures. Classically based architecture bristled with aspiration—order and symmetry celebrated civic, political, and military ideals, a message that co-opted the creative imagination of the fledgling United States. As for prototypical site-specific and culture-specific dwellings—their significance for the architectural lineage of the Americas was blotted out for centuries.

Everywhere, that is, except New Mexico. Rather than being marginalized, the pueblo style has been canonized. Characterized by thick adobe walls of earth, water, and straw, it embodies the popular conception of Santa Fe architectural style. Pink, tan, or brown adobe dwellings are cozily at home in this high desert setting. Portals or porches stretch across fronts, sides, and backs of the structures and make welcoming outside places for residents to dine and relax and still be protected from the harsh sun. The popularity of pueblo architecture was assured when it became the official Santa Fe style, largely due to the efforts of one architect. John Gaw Meem's impact on the city of Santa Fe can't be overstated. The architect designed many of the city's most memorable buildings including the Museum of International Folk Art and an addition to the La Fonda Hotel, and he also headed the committee that wrote the 1957 Historical Zoning Ordinance ensuring that all future buildings in central Santa Fe adhere to the vernacular idioms of the Old Quarter.

Even before Meem, though, stylistic modifications to pueblo architecture were a handy way to normalize political shifts. After New Mexico became a U.S. territory in 1846, it quickly became fashionable to retrofit the windows and doors of existing adobe buildings with Federal-style trim painted white or turquoise. White

The White House Ruin is one of the most dramatic of the cliff dwellings built by the Ancestral Puebloans in Canyon de Chelly National Monument. The Puebloans began to vacate the canyons around 1300, but today Canyon de Chelly sits in the middle of the Navajo Nation and is still home to many Navajo.

Georgia O'Keeffe's Abiquiu house is built around a central patio, which is approached through a zaguan. Her spare bedroom receives abundant light through windows across from the bed. They offered her a view of the road to Espanola, Santa Fe, and "the world," as she put it.

Doric columns replaced tree trunk columns to support portals and porches. The after-market additions were stylistic shorthand that implied acquiescence to a new reality.

The territory of New Mexico became a state in 1912 and was still considered exotic when arts patron Mabel Dodge Luhan settled in Taos in 1917. New Mexico modernism today is the aesthetic descendant of a community of iconoclastic artists who made their way to the state at her invitation. Those artists included Marsden Hartley, John Marin, Stuart Davis, Arnold Rónnebeck and Louise Emerson Rónnebeck, and Georgia O'Keeffe. They were enthralled by the sun-drenched landscape of the Southwest and its range of saturated colors, especially the bright blue sky, the pinks and purples at sunset, and the pinks and greens of the land and vegetation. They were radical artists who also understood that the New Mexico terrain invited fresh modernist interpretations that, particularly in Georgia O'Keeffe's work, inspired a framework for an exploration of color and shape.

Not all of these artists remained in New Mexico, but Georgia O'Keeffe did. She first came to New Mexico in 1917 when she spent a few days in Santa Fe. She returned to paint in 1929. In 1940 the artist bought Ghost Ranch after living in it for a few years; she purchased the house in Abiquiu in 1945. Ghost Ranch— an adobe territorial pueblo style with square columns and window and door trim--was relatively new. O'Keeffe gently renovated Ghost Ranch by removing a small double-hung window in her studio and replacing it with a six-paned picture window that admitted north light; she also streamlined the north side of the house by eliminating the ends of the support beams (vigas) as well as the downspouts, or canales. In her bedroom two picture windows butt together at the corner, suggesting mitering, a strategy modernist architects such as Frank Lloyd Wright employed to allow unobstructed views. Also in O'Keeffe's bedroom, a Calder mobile is suspended over the bed; her painting *My Last Door* takes command of the east wall. The Abiquiu house is even sparer. A humble twin bed draped in white linens

seems monastic. On the ledge above the bed, rocks and seashells are a distillation of the artist's instinct for form and contour. With these modest gestures modernist interior design and architecture quietly made their way into New Mexico.

In the last two decades, a robust proliferation of modernist homes has changed both the shape and the intention of buildings and their relationship to the surrounding landscape. The dramatic high desert is the perfect setting for bold, abstracted forms found in modernist houses, each a reflection of the other's shape. These houses provide a way to evoke a sense of place. Wide swaths of glass, deep-set portals, long porches, and courtyards allow vistas, color, and light to become integral to the very being of a house, enabling a way to experience the world outside and still be safe.

The architects featured in this book take their vocabulary from the New Mexico landscape, reinforcing what is apparent—that this is the only way modernism can make sense in the harsh and arid climate. They defer to basic materials such as adobe and wood, in combination with steel and glass, and apply this language to the meticulous convictions of modernism. Several houses are rusted Corten steel, its reddish hue blending into the surrounding terrain; others are concrete, stucco, or adobe (two incorporate an older adobe structure); still others are stacked rock, reminiscent of the structures built against the cliffs at Canyon de Chelly in Arizona, Chaco Canyon in New Mexico, Mesa Verde in Colorado, and Hovenweep National Monument in Colorado and Utah.

But most importantly, these houses—although they refer to another time—are very much of the here and now. They count on the elemental integrity of old building traditions while at the same time asserting a way of life that worked in the past, that works in the present, and that will work in the future. The houses represent a revelation of the rightness of context (of which Santa Fe is the quintessential example), where communities—both of people and of dwellings— are an incarnation of our longing to be part of the world around and above us.

Core

Gallerist Max Protetch made a name for himself in the art world by finding value where none was perceived. Protetch maximized the market for architectural drawings, which he sold from the eponymous gallery he opened in 1969 while he was a graduate student in political science at Georgetown University. Over the next forty years, Protetch showed works by many of architecture's greatest stars at his New York gallery: Frank Gehry, Robert Venturi, Michael Graves, Rem Koolhaas, Zaha Hadid, Tadao Ando, and Samuel Mockbee, among others. Similarly, his wife, Irene Hofmann, has spent her professional life promoting the work of contemporary art and artists as a curator at the Cranbrook Art Museum, director of the Contemporary Museum in Baltimore, and, from 2010 until 2020, as director and chief curator of the contemporary art space SITE Santa Fe.

The couple's house in Santa Fe is exactly the kind of place two people who relish discovery would be inhabiting. When Hofmann accepted the position at SITE Santa Fe, Protetch assumed he'd visit her and live in Santa Fe part-time. But—"just for fun," he says—the indefatigable explorer started looking for houses. While driving around the southern outskirts of town, Protetch saw a "For Sale" sign, turned onto a side road, and navigated his car up the rocky lane, passing through a gate and pushing ahead until he arrived at the ranch-style midcentury structure. Clad in gray clapboard with a flourish of Territorial style in the white trim on the windows and the portal, the house was built in the 1970s by William R. Buckley, a colleague of Santa Fe architect John Gaw Meem. The house butts up against a cliff on one side, but on the other, it opens wide to an expansive view of the Jemez and Sandia Mountains. As Protetch investigated the interior spaces, he descended a steep staircase into a subterranean room. There, he opened door after door until he arrived at one smaller than the others. "What's behind this?" he asked. Looking inside, he came face-to-face with the intact granite outcropping against which the entire house was built. Shockingly immediate, the brown, gray, and gold cliffside was a revelation of the minutia of the surrounding landscape. "That's why I bought the house," says Protetch.

Hofmann and Protetch collaborated with the Santa Fe-based architecture firm Suby Bowden & Associates on a counterintuitive design to streamline the two-story, four-bedroom residence into a one-bedroom house—recasting the entire lower story as a principal bedroom and bath. At the top of the staircase, a bedroom became Hofmann's dressing room and bath. When the walls of the third and fourth bedrooms on the other side of the house were demolished, the space unfurled into a second living and dining area. But most conspicuously, the drywall downstairs was removed, and Protetch (then 65), armed with a jackhammer and three days' worth of lessons on how to use it, chiseled out several tons of rock to clear the way for the new principal bedroom and bath.

By removing walls, the couple freed up space to display paintings, photographs, and drawings from Protetch's collection. "I brought in most of the furniture," says Hofmann, whose personal collection of first-edition pieces such as the 1956 gateleg birch dining table by Bruno Mathsson and accompanying Eames chairs attests to her taste as well as her tenure at the Cranbrook Art Museum, considered the birthplace of midcentury design in America.

Now, the couple lives in the midst of both the avant-garde and the ancient. The panorama from the living room and their bedroom is the mountains, but the view that's the most engaging is the monumental rock wall. It is the core of the house, dominating an entire side of the bedroom and visible from every vantage point in the house. The wall is more than a remnant from the beginning of time; it is very much still alive, mottled with lichen that's dried to a crusty gold. As inhabitants of this eccentric house Protetch and Hofmann are always reminded that the place they occupy is in a landscape that is both exquisite in detail and sumptuous from afar: Without the landscape the house is nothing. It is a fact that never fails to inspire both Protetch and Hofmann. "This is a place," Hofmann says, "where we can think and be creative."

William R. Buckley

Values

PREVIOUS PAGES AND RIGHT:
In one of the two dining areas, Iñigo Manglano-Ovalle's *Cloud Prototype No. 2* hovers over a Fritz Hansen lounge chair. Eames chairs and a custom bench accompany the 1956 Bruno Mathsson gateleg table. The timber ceiling and beams are original to the house; Protetch and Hofmann added the scored concrete floors.

Core Values

OPPOSITE: *Synecdoche*, a 96-panel portrait recording each sitter's skin tone, hangs above the sofa in the family room; artist Byron Kim considers it an ongoing project. The Womb chair is by Eero Saarinen and the ottoman is from Knoll.
ABOVE: Between the kitchen and the living area, a second dining table is flanked by four vintage chrome-and-leather art deco chairs. Beyond are Marilyn Minter's *Dogs from Hell* and Tobias Putrih's cardboard sculpture *Macula*.

17

ABOVE: A salon hanging in the hallway features drawings by leading twentieth-century architects; above the door is a drawing by Wallace K. Harrison of the U.N. General Assembly building. OPPOSITE: The wood-burning stove is in the heart of the house, surrounded by the kitchen, the family room, and the dining room. Fixtures include a Louis Poulsen pendant over the dining table and pendants and sconces from a 1950s design used as task lighting in the kitchen.

OPPOSITE: *Landscape Series* by Lu Wei hangs in the stairwell, viewed best from across the space. BELOW: In the principal bedroom, a vintage black-leather Le Corbusier chaise longue finds its spot between the rock wall and artist Scott Burton's plywood tripod table.

The black steel staircase, built by local welder Larry Swan, seems to emerge out of the granite outcropping. Its precise sculptural presence contrasts with the elemental power of the rock. The matte black ceiling complements the effect. In the bedroom, a trio of photographs by Yang Zhenzhong—*The Nuclear Family*, *The Old Days*, and *One Child Family*—hangs above the bed.

View

Sky

In Tesuque, a glass, rusted corrugated Corten steel, and light gray stucco house slotted between low-lying Sugar Loaf Mountain and the upper reaches of the Santa Fe National Forest in the distance offers its owners all the advantages—and none of the disadvantages—of year-round living on a porch. Although Tesuque seems remote, the village is only six miles north of Santa Fe's downtown plaza and just south of the Tesuque Pueblo. Mark Wellen, an architect based in Midland, Texas, designed the house for a couple who moved to New Mexico from Midland with their two young daughters in 2012.

"This house," says Wellen, "opens to the sky on both sides." But the sky views are the antithesis of the predictable Santa Fe views. "Instead of facing west to catch the sunset, the site gave us only one option, and that was to face north," he explains. For optimal viewing, a forty-four-foot expanse of double-height glass creates a porch-like living and dining space that's bathed in northern light during the day and open to the stars at night. Steel-framed doors on both sides slide wide to invite the outdoors into the airy room.

"We open them completely in the summer," says the husband, an energy consultant; his wife is a retired broadcast journalist.

Wellen's design directs all private activities to the two-story stucco boxes that firmly clasp the house's airy midsection like bookends. The box on the left houses kitchen, principal bedroom, and upstairs office and the box on the right holds the daughters' bedrooms and baths. In the winter, the flanking wings seem to rise out of the snow, taking on the color of hunks of ice. In front, a covered porch overlooks two concrete terraces that lead from the driveway to the house, positioning itself as a grandstand for viewing the Sangre de Cristo Mountains ten miles away as the crow flies. That view is where the showmanship occurs. Everyone in Santa Fe is entranced by the sunset, but here, the light from the setting sun saturates the mountains, cloaking them in pinks and purples that, in the fall, reach psychedelic splendor as they commingle with the shimmering golds of the aspen trees. In the owners' opinion nothing else can compare. "This is the reason," they say, "that we decided not to have any art in our house."

PAGES 22–23: Porches extend the full length of the living space on both sides of the house. Waxed hand-troweled concrete floors and cement board ceiling panels link the interior space to the porches; dark charcoal gravel in the courtyard complements the black steel framed windows and doors. PRECEDING PAGES: The two-bedroom guesthouse is a shipping container topped with a cantilevered Corten shed roof. Gabion walls made from rubble on the building site provide drainage and erosion control. RIGHT: A plaster-clad Rumford fireplace separates the dining and living rooms. The longleaf pine table was designed by Mark Wellen; the side chairs are Bertoia for Knoll.

Sky View

OPPOSITE: On the front porch, the Corten canopy thrusts upward at a 15-degree angle to open views of the ski basin. It is supported by thin steel pipes similar to oil field pipe and familiar to the owners who are in the oil business. ABOVE: Wellen made liberal use of corrugated Corten steel throughout this project as a way of integrating the house with the surrounding rust-colored terrain.

Pueblo Revival

On February 9, 1880, the first train pulled into the Santa Fe, New Mexico, depot. Its arrival spelled the demise of the old Santa Fe Trail (the route still exists as a street that meanders through the city). It was a treacherous rutted thoroughfare but essential for commerce between Franklin, Missouri, and Santa Fe. The advent of the railroad—with its sleeping cars and dining rooms—introduced the idea that traveling was fun, and tourists flocked to the exotic city. The railway station has now been repurposed as the Railyard, an arts district that is still a vital part of Santa Fe life.

It also spawned the development of nearby neighborhoods. The South Capitol neighborhood is one of those, where Victorian, Territorial-style, and Pueblo Revival-style houses sit on tree-lined streets outlined by sidewalks. It was through this neighborhood that Lauren Hunt often drove, just to get a glimpse of her favorite house. The adobe residence built in 1929 sits back from the street on three-quarters of an acre, its quiet poise deriving from the elegance of the Pueblo Revival style architecture. A wide portal connects to two square volumes on either side—one with an expanse of white-trimmed mullioned windows; the other with a single Territorial-style window peaked at the top like the pediment of a tiny Greek temple. The extra-cultural flourish is a tip of the hat to an architectural moment between 1850 and 1912 when New Mexico was still a territory, and wood had become available as a building material.

The house had beguiled both Lauren and her husband, Brad, and when it came on the market, they made an offer. "I bought the big black cupboard that is now in the dining room just for this house even though we didn't own it yet," says Lauren. But she anticipated living there. With its rational floor plan—three bedrooms down a long hall (the interior mate to the portal outside) and the living room, dining room, and kitchen on the right—the house invited gracious living. "I based my decision on the way this house made me feel—grounded and very supported," she said.

That feeling wasn't achieved by accident. The serene residence was designed by John Gaw Meem, best known for his pivotal role in the development of the Pueblo Revival style in the Southwest. Meem was doing at the time what a few other architects were doing (notably in Texas)—he looked to the international modernist movement, reinterpreting it with his own version that was suitable to his region's environment and history.

Meem used the past for reference, but his work has the clarity and elegance associated with modernism. His architectural touch is deceptively simple and relies on complex infrastructure for gravitas. It was a subtlety that Lauren Hunt responded to. She is the owner of Hunt Modern, a Santa Fe gallery specializing in European twentieth-century design. But the midcentury advocate especially relishes championing the influence of modernism on the Pueblo Revival aesthetic. She and Brad have filled the house with well-crafted examples of modern design. Pieces by Finn Juhl, Hans Wegner, Pierre Jeanneret, and George Nakashima seem richly evocative in the comfortable setting, their craft a domestic inflection of the craft inherent in Meem's work.

"Modernism," Hunt says, "is informed by the maker." The Nakashima credenza, dining table, and stool in her house exemplify the humanity inherent in midcentury furniture. "If we don't have a big George Nakashima piece in the studio," she notes, "I can feel it." Meem's pared-down version of Pueblo-style architecture suggests that he was thinking about traditional building in a way that was unconventional for the time in which he worked. Legions of latter-day imitators have meant that the architect's contrarian views are routinely misinterpreted. But not by Hunt. "The spaces in this house have a magical modern feeling," says his admirer. "I think of Meem as an early modernist in the Southwest."

PRECEDING PAGES: Lauren Hunt designed the minimalist landscape and the stone wall, emphasizing existing sharp lines to give the house a modern feeling. OPPOSITE: The whimsical chair was recently identified as a Clam chair by the little-known Danish designer Philip Arctander.

In the living room, the Hunts retained
the original mullioned windows
and the pine plank ceiling and vigas.
A glass chandelier by Mauri Almari
hangs above the Jumbo marble coffee
table by Gae Aulenti; facing it are
two Henning Kjaernulf Razor Blade oak
chairs. Near the fireplace is a grass-
seated Nakashima stool.

OPPOSITE: The mohair velvet sofa is by Danish designer Illum Wikkelsø. On the wall is a pair of Piedra sconces in travertine by L'Aviva Home. ABOVE: The Seguso scavo Murano glass vases on the Axel Einar Hjorth bureau are part of Lauren Hunt's collection; the lamp is by Gordon Martz.

The dining room features the Danish ebonized wood cupboard, 1627, that Lauren Hunt purchased specifically for the house. To the left is a stoneware vase by Claude Conover. The pine floors are original but now stained ebony, a dramatic contrast to the white plaster walls. The Nakashima table is surrounded by Kai Christensen chairs upholstered in leather. All are illuminated by a brass and opaline-glass Stilnovo pendant.

OPPOSITE: Jasper Johns's lithograph *Flag (Moratorium)*, 1969, is the focal point of the hall. On the right is an Italian bench and above a light fixture by Finnish artist Paavo Tynell, both from the 1940s. The rug is an early twentieth-century Gabbeh kilim. ABOVE: A painting by Barbara Cathcart hangs above the De La Espada bed. The cane chair is from Hunt Modern's Chandigarh line, re-editions of midcentury designs for the Indian planned city.

On
the

To get to Eddie Nunns's house you must drive along a road that winds up and down hills until it abruptly stops, as if you have come to the last remaining inches on the globe. Spread before you is an 180-degree panorama, a barren pink-tinged landscape that overlooks Los Alamos and the steep canyons that cut between the mesa on which Nunns's house sits.

Tucked behind a hillock on the right is the house, a procession of refined boxy volumes that reinterpret the craggy terrain beyond. Nunns has been in Santa Fe since 2007—the Texas native's life dream. "I came here when I was five for a summer vacation with my parents," he says. "This is summer? I thought. No mosquitoes, no humidity. I'm going to live here someday."

Decades passed before the dream became reality. For more than thirty years Nunns worked for Neiman Marcus, capping his career there as vice president of creative services and brand steward. When the fashion influencer retired from a job that focused on glamour and glitz, he needed the opposite in his new life: "I wanted a minimalist home and barren expanses." Nunns sought advice from Santa Fe architect Trey Jordan. Presented with the lot Nunns had found, Jordan observed, "We'll have to cut the top of the hill off to get your house in there."

Fifteen feet of soil was removed from the top of the hill to make a flat place to build the stucco, steel, and glass house. The drastic move left the site intentionally exposed to the dramatic setting, as if it were alone on a precipice. "We created a very strong sense of edge that strengthened the already existing feeling that Eddie was on the border of the rest of the world," Jordan explains. He tempered the startling juxtaposition with a series of enclosed spaces that buffer the house from its environment, starting with a courtyard embraced by stucco walls.

"I thought about the opposing view, which is open, and I wanted to contrast it with the enclosed spaces around the house," says Jordan. The house embodies a strong reference to pueblo architecture. "I wanted it to look like horizontal hunks on the ground," he says. The structure seems to have alighted on its site in a sequence—a rhythm that relieves the house of the bulkiness characteristic of pueblo buildings. "The massing is broken up like chunks of buildings so that it isn't monolithic," Jordan explains. "It's what makes modern work in a place like this."

The entry courtyard has the effect of disconnecting context, making a private world through which all must pass, almost as if it's a ceremony to approach the steps that lead to the front door. "It's one long gesture," says Jordan. "I removed everything from the entry gate so that it's quiet and still—and then you rediscover the inside."

"Trey's signature," says Nunns, "is that he often does a room within a room so that the interior room seems to float in the larger space." Here, the interior box—lacquered a velvety gray—anchors the main building. Glossy and mysterious, the box is like a pillar around which the other spaces circulate—living room, dining room, and kitchen form an L around the front of the box; from the kitchen, a back hallway leads to a guest bedroom and makes a turn into another hallway that rejoins the living room.

The light-filled house has another personality at night. A picture window in the living room faces northeast; at night it's animated by the twinkling lights from Los Alamos thirty-four miles northwest. The house, peaceful by day, seems to be amused by a little secret at night, no longer looking out onto a barren prospect but onto the sparkling and somewhat enigmatic panorama that excites the black New Mexico nights.

Verge

PRECEDING PAGES: Architect Trey Jordan designed the courtyard so that the concrete steps to the front door are sheltered by a floating steel-framed roof above the garage. OPPOSITE: Diamond-finish plaster walls in the living room reflect the ambient light. James Havard's *Rembrandt van Rijn* hangs above the fireplace; the extended concrete hearth is a favorite place to sit. ABOVE: Sliding glass doors open onto the front courtyard and minimalist koi pond. To the left a charcoal and pierced-paper collage of a black crow by James Drake sits on a midcentury credenza.

PRECEDING PAGES: Retracting glass doors in the living room look out onto the rear patio and the landscape to the north. The pieced-cowhide rug is by Kyle Bunting and the Minotti sofa and chair are from Smink. ABOVE AND OPPOSITE: The living and dining rooms wrap around an enclosed central element that houses functional spaces. Lacquered a dark gray, it has niche for an inset credenza, which displays a time-bleached antler amid pieces of black micaceous clay cookware. The photograph is by Jeff Stephens.

OPPOSITE: A small fireplace is recessed into an angled wall in the principal bedroom. A muted gray palette—concrete floors, natural-colored plaster, and plywood panel ceilings and vigas painted a soft putty color—signals serenity. ABOVE: Concrete steps lead up from the entry of the enclosed courtyard and main house, tucked away behind a 9-foot-tall walnut door—its high and narrow proportions suggesting a little mystery.

In the Spirit

Linda Lynch's stucco house resembles an unadorned triptych, the three pavilions attached at 45-degree angles as if perfectly positioned on a landscaped-sized altar. This is not far from the truth, for the house faces an area considered to be sacred. It sits at the end of a winding rocky road and is open on the rear to the prospect twenty miles east of the magnificent Galisteo Basin, one of the most impressive archeological sites in the United States. There is more obvious drama above, though, and Lynch, an artist, often watches from her living room window as black rolling clouds of fierce storms tumble across the big horizon.

The front of Lynch's house has a quiet and respectful mien, appropriate to its location directly in front of Mount Chaclchihuiti, a short stroll to the west. A sacred place for the Pueblo people (there are nineteen pueblos near Santa Fe), it is the point of emergence for one of their ancestral spirits, or kachina, the Turquoise Lady. Mount Chalchihuiti is the site of numerous prehistoric turquoise mines, which probably supplied much of the turquoise used in pre-Spanish times— no other sources are known. But later history has been unkind to the little mountain, now just on the other side of Lynch's property line. In the 1600s, the Spaniards marched up from Mexico to claim the mines for themselves. Around 1900, a company associated with Tiffany & Co. bought the mines. Tiffany used the turquoise in jewelry, eventually depleting the entire supply. The coup de grâce was delivered by a gravel company that strip-mined the mountain, scattering gravel and tiny pieces of turquoise along what is now State Highway 14 just below Lynch's house. The road is now paved with the tailings of the blue-green mineral.

Linda Lynch's house gazes thoughtfully at the former mine and incorporates its dignity of place into its general outlook. The building was designed by architect Elisabeth Wagner, then in Santa Fe, for a marketing executive for Warner Bros. He prized the location and wanted to make it even more special, specifying that the middle pavilion align with the winter solstice. On December 21, the light coming through the living room window hits the original owner's mirror hanging above the fireplace. "The location and the landscape are so breathtaking," says Lynch, "that it made me want to live here, even though I wasn't planning to move or to buy a house." She had restored a historic hotel near the Texas border not far from El Paso, where she worked on her art projects. Although it was isolated, her home was near where she and her two sisters grew up, on a ranch in the Chihuahuan Desert. And there she had intended to stay. Lynch changed her mind after her sister Bonnie saw that this house was for sale, and the pair visited it. Some things about the house and its setting reminded her of the desert where she grew up. There, as in New Mexico, the land and the sky are showy parallel universes of ever-evolving drama, color, and texture. The splendor never fails to enthrall, and especially here in her Santa Fe house: "Every single moment the view is different," says Lynch.

The house is lucidly symmetrical: A wide entrance hallway ushers guests into the middle pavilion where a compact galley kitchen, open on both ends, precedes the living and dining room. To the right, a pavilion holds the principal bedroom and bath; the third is Lynch's office. The artist has filled all the spaces with her art as well as artifacts collected in her wide-ranging travels. It's a quiet place, befitting the location in the shadow of a sacred mountain still visited by Pueblo Indians, who enter the precinct through a gate in Lynch's fence. The house exudes the jewel-like incandescence of the surrounding sand and grit and owes its radiance to floors made from hand-honed pink Turkish onyx. Presumably precious and not particularly durable, these floors have held up over the years and reinforce the impression of otherworldliness that permeates Linda Lynch's private world.

Hans Wegner chairs accompany the dining table, originally a French cloth-cutting table. *Barque*, a pastel pigment drawing by Linda Lynch, hangs behind it.

A Senufo Ivory Coast ceremonial
bed becomes a coffee table that
displays a processional puppet from
Mali. An Ashanti stool doubles as a
footrest, while an Ethiopian tri-legged
stool is a convenient side table.
The runner is Iranian, the mate of the
one under the dining table.

OPPOSITE: A Dogon ladder has impressive sculptural presence in the entry hall, lit by alabaster sconces designed by architect Elisabeth Wagner. Lynch acquired the Ethiopian chair on her travels. BELOW: Lynch displays other pieces from her collection in her bedroom including a Kuba cloth remnant and an Ethiopian chair. An Ivory Coast indigo textile is stretched across the end of the bed.

About   Light

and   Time

In northern New Mexico, the ancient is ever present, a fact that was much on the mind of New York-based architect Mark DuBois when he looked for the best way to site the house he was designing for Jeanne and Michael Klein. The couple spends a lot of time outdoors, and they are also avid art collectors with an impressive holding of paintings, drawings, sculpture, and video works. They wanted to build a modern glass house in the desert that afforded them a constant view of nature and that also was a place where they could display art. After a long search for land, they fell in love with and chose twenty rugged acres that back up to a national forest north of Santa Fe, remembered now as the bishop's "little country estate" in Willa Cather's 1927 novel *Death Comes for the Archbishop*. The only buildable place, it became obvious, was a gentle ridge that slopes away from the mountain on three sides. DuBois did not want the house to dominate the landscape, and accordingly he embedded the basalt, concrete, and glass building three feet down so as not to overtop the pines.

The building is organized as a series of unpunctured concrete walls—a tribute to the series of parallel steel walls in the Richard Serra installation at La Mormaire near Paris. Serra's walls channel movement and views through a garden; Dubois's walls do the same. In this mountainous setting, three stone- and glass-walled pavilions emerge from the house: one is a 150-foot-long main space for living, flanked by a principal bedroom and the garage, and a three-bedroom guest wing. The roof heights of the pavilions follow the grade change of the hill beneath, and the house seems at one with its setting.

Even before construction began, works by Ellsworth Kelly, John Chamberlain, Kiki Smith, Richard Serra, and Donald Judd were situated on-site, anticipating where they would be permanently installed once the house was completed. In the middle of it all, and a floor below, a James Turrell *Skyspace* was sunk into in the center of the house; through its square aperture the sky and light provide much to contemplate. Inside, too, there is the man-made to consider. The living room, for instance, was sized to accommodate a particularly large Ellsworth Kelly painting. DuBois was committed to providing enough space for both the art and the view to be appreciated: "Creating a sense of openness was something the house demanded," he explains. It was a demand that elicited an unprecedented response from the architect. The exterior walls of the living room are made of structural glass uninterrupted by columns and bearing the weight of the thick slab roof.

The house is a collaboration between air and earth, and pavilions and courtyards seem to have emerged from the landscape, just as elemental although more composed. "It was fundamental," says DuBois, "to have that sense of connection to the land." The Kleins have a significant collection of site-specific pieces by Olafur Eliasson and Andy Goldsworthy, but architect DuBois intentionally avoided designing their house as if it were a site-specific piece of art. It is part of the terrain, and as such is a rich backdrop for the art both inside and outside the house. Paula Hayes designed the landscape around the house, blurring the distinction between art and nature.

Studio DuBois

OPPOSITE: A mid-twentieth-century perforated bamboo form sits on the Nakashima dining table, lit by ceramic fixtures by Jo Whiting. The leather chairs are by Vladimir Kagan. BELOW: Random length slabs of basaltine are polished to a mirror finish in the hall leading to the principal suite. Transparency contrasts with texture, with a glass wall facing stacked slices of American walnut.

The waxed zinc fireplace commands the space, dividing dining from living rooms. The furniture grouping features a Nakashima coffee table and a pair of Vladimir Kagan Contour lounge chairs flanking a Serge Mouille floor lamp from the 1930s. Delicate cables of colored yarn by Fred Sandback stretch across both rooms.

ABOVE: Outside the principal suite, the hallway becomes a gallery for a diverse collection of art including works by Gerhard Richter and Cindy Sherman. OPPOSITE: In the principal bedroom, the furniture merges with the architecture as the basaltine steps incorporate the custom bed and nightstand. Donald Judd's large-scale wall piece *Bullnose* hangs on the concrete wall above. Two works on paper entitled *Composition* are by Nadezhda Udalzawa.

BELOW: In the library, an iconic black-leather Eames lounge chair and ottoman are surrounded by collections of Japanese bamboo art and Martin Brothers ceramic vessels. OPPOSITE: A James Turrell *Skyspace* occupies the center of the house; entered from the lower level, the teak-lined space opens to the sky's ever-evolving moods.

Cubist

In Santa Fe stunning views are ubiquitous—even, perhaps, hard to avoid. Mountains loom in the distance, Technicolor sunrises and sunsets always thrill, and puffy clouds crowd the crisply blue sky. But San Antonio-based architect Ted Flato of Lake | Flato Architects dodged the temptation to overdose on obvious abundance with this compound built around a courtyard. The adobe and Corten house initially ignores the views, substituting an interior field of vision that serves as the entry and the heart of the residence. It's bordered by a flagstone porch, an open-air passage along two sides of the courtyard that leads to the front door opposite the entry gate. Beyond the door, at the end of the entry hall, a floor-to-ceiling window reveals desert expanse.

The house belongs to Sally and Tom Dunning. Both are civic activists in Dallas; she is also an interior designer. The Santa Fe property is a retreat the couple shares with their family and friends.

From the front the house looks like a simple square—an elegant reference to Spanish Pueblo Revival design, where a courtyard is the organizing element of the plan. Here the traditional simplicity unfolds into well-orchestrated complexity. "We thought of the house as a series of six solid cubes with open ends," says Flato, "so that the exterior of the house looks outward in all directions."

The six "cubes" were inspired by Donald Judd's minimalist concrete boxes at the Chinati Foundation in Marfa. They are arranged around the courtyard, each housing a separate function: living/dining space, kitchen and garage, principal suite and three guest suites. Glazed openings between cubes create all-weather porches.

Inside, the atmosphere is as muted as a Spanish mission. "We thought of this house in terms of how you would experience light inside," says Flato. The light is palpable, as much an element of the architecture as are the plastered adobe walls. It arrives via a deep-set window and high windows at the far end of the living room and filters across the walls to the living and dining rooms. The window frames a close-up view of the desert by day; by night the lights of Los Alamos twinkle in the distance. Calm prevails, and the building's sensuality overtakes all distractions. The senses matter here, and it's possible to see, feel, and hear as if those sensations are completely new. "We can hear the sounds of the aspen leaves rustling in the fall, see how the breezes blow in the summer, and watch the light through the louvered slats during the day," says Sally.

Movement

PRECEDING PAGES: Mixed-color waxed plaster walls in the living room have
a cloud-like effect, a contrast to the rusted steel in the fireplace and the rolling
screen designed by San Antonio metal artist Cactus Max Patino. Vintage
and contemporary coexist in the space. The chair, from a private yacht, was
purchased by Sally Dunning at a Santa Fe yard sale; the sofa belonged
to her mother. On the walls are works by Robert Kelly, Margeaux, and Joel
Shapiro. OPPOSITE: The kitchen is the essence of efficiency paired with glamour,
thanks to a marble waterfall island and a back-lit frosted glass backsplash.
ABOVE: Archival pigment prints by Erin Shirreff hang in the front entry.

ABOVE: An abstract work by Robert Kelly overlooks the dining table, designed by Sir Norman Foster, where contemporary Japanese bamboo art is displayed. Over the sliding doors opening to the courtyard is a group of geometric prints by Sol LeWitt.
OPPOSITE: A tapestry with cowrie shells hangs above the custom bed in the principal bedroom; next to it a delicate bamboo ladder becomes a sculpture propped against the wall.

OPPOSITE: A rusted steel slatted gate opens into the courtyard, which is framed on all sides by a portal that provides both shade and the pathway into the house and its flanking guest rooms. The circular fiberglass forms are by David Henderson. ABOVE: Pine ceilings and rusted steel beams are a modern version of the viga and latilla ceilings of traditional adobe architecture. The white wall sculpture is by Ted Larsen. OVERLEAF: The solid cubes pierced by window walls and the glazed connectors epitomize the contemporary reinterpretation of traditional pueblo architecture. The division of the windows into segments framing a part of the view makes the vastness of the desert more manageable when seen from within.

Digging

Deep

In 2006 a Dallas couple visiting Santa Fe took a realtor up on his offer to show them what he called "the best view in town." The destination—a narrow lot about midway up a hillside that is, at 7,650 feet, the city's highest elevation—lived up to the hype. The rock outcrop overlooks the Jemez Mountains, and more. "You can see the Badlands in Arizona," says the husband, referring to an otherworldly area where wind and water have eroded soft sedimentary rock and clay-rich soil into wave-like gullies, steep slopes, and odd silhouettes richly stratified with bands of varying shades of gray and red rock. It's a stunning sight from a distance of about 420 miles away.

"This is where I want to spend the rest of my life," said the husband, a retired entrepreneur. Although he and his wife, an education consultant, hadn't been ready to commit to a move, they changed their minds when they saw the lot and purchased it immediately. They then hired Austin-based architect Larry Speck, former dean of the University of Texas School of Architecture and principal at the design firm Page, to design a house for the escarpment. Speck was intrigued by the complexity of the craggy site: "It was quite difficult to make it work because there weren't any flat areas."

The contour of the landscape came to define the understated profile of the house—at 172 feet, it's more than three times as long as it is wide. So, too, did it influence the materials—cement, ipe wood, glass, and rammed earth. "It was all about the site," says Speck, who was captivated by the layers of pink-and-brown sedimentary rock that make the mountains around Santa Fe, especially near Abiquiu, look vibrantly striped.

"I loved the way the layers of color in those hills marked the horizontality of the landscape," he continues.

The terrain's joyous linearity was Speck's reason for using rammed earth for the two walls that cut the long, narrow house into thirds, separating guest space in front from the main living space in the middle and from the glass-walled principal suite in the back. Rammed earth is a building process used in the Desert Southwest because it creates a high thermal mass similar to adobe. It has an ancient history: Jericho, history's earliest known city, was built of earth. Parts of the Great Wall of China are also built of rammed earth.

Inspired by the kaleidoscopic variety of colors in the area, Speck arranged for his rammed earth walls to be as extravagantly composed: extending from the back porch, through the house, and out onto the front porch, the two partitions are a melange of browns, beiges, pinks, terra-cottas, and reds that evoke the earthy opulence of Santa Fe. An abstract partition of metal tiles takes the palette of the rammed earth wall one step further, incorporating primary colors from the sky, the light, the sunsets.

"We wanted it to seem like the architecture grew out of the landscape," says Speck. In this case, the landscape also grows out of the architecture. The husband is an avid horticulturalist, and in addition to a narrow garden along the back of the house, he has planted the 3,000-square-foot roof with wildflowers. Beyond its function as a water retention network that channels all rain into a catchment system, the roof enhances the view for neighbors farther up the mountain.

The rock outcrop against which the house is built is a major presence in the narrow and sunny garden. On the street side, the building lies long and low, virtually invisible from all approaches. In materials and form, the house reflects the modest profiles of pueblo architecture.

Texture plays an important role in this house: local gravel was added to the concrete mix for the floors, which are diamond-finished. Four shades of the indigenous sedimentary dirt in the rammed earth walls create a deep, variegated palette that resonates with the broader terrain. The ipe ceiling extends into the garden where it becomes a generous overhang.

93

Installation artist Margo Sawyer created *Synchronicity of Color*, panels that wrap around the service core in the middle of the living area. The surfaces of the square and rectangular forms reflect light variously, creating an intermediate zone between the matte gray of the kitchen cabinets and island and the striated hues in the rammed earth wall.

94

When Santa Fe–based architect Robert Zachry was a youngster in the late 1940s and 1950s, his parents would pile the family in the car for the cross-country trek from Los Angeles to Texarkana, Texas, to visit relatives. They always stopped midway in Santa Fe. The trip did something momentous for the young Zachry: "It made me want to live in Santa Fe, which was the most beautiful place I had ever seen." Zachry also had youthful aspirations to become a car designer. Instead, he ventured into the slightly more practical field of architecture, apprenticing with Cesar Pelli and Anthony Lumsden, both known for their futuristic, often sculptural, building designs.

In 1984 Zachry made it back to Santa Fe, where he has lived ever since. He always designed modern houses, even when there wasn't much demand for them. Despite that, modern houses in an ancient topography made sense to him. Big glass walls, wide portals, and outdoor spaces offered a magnanimous way to merge a house into the landscape. The steel, stucco, and glass house where two patrons of the arts now live is a pithy expression of Zachry's opinion, focusing on a view west and south toward both the Jemez Mountains and the Santa Fe city lights. The warehouse-like structure seems to recede into the rock face of the foothills behind it, its glass-walled facade favoring the substantial structure with a sense of transparency.

The homeowners are both from Antwerp, via Columbus, Georgia, where the husband was CEO of the W.C. Bradley Co., a company focused on home and leisure products and services. The wife is the chair of SITE Santa Fe, a contemporary art space. "We both grew up surrounded by art," he says about their young lives in Belgium where fine art, religious art, tribal art, modern art, fashion, design, and architecture are enriching components of everyday Belgian life. "It is part of our DNA," notes the wife. The couple had renovated an 1880s-era cotton mill in Columbus, where they lived before moving to Santa Fe. They filled the huge space with modern art, and when they found the Santa Fe house, its enormous, light-filled living space—just slightly smaller than a professional basketball court—offered the same kind of convivial setting for their art to show to its best advantage.

The approach to the one-story dwelling wedged halfway up a steep slope is similar to the climb up to an inaccessible religious site, the implication being that heaven is hard to reach. In this case, though, terrace-like limestone steps make it easier, and the reward is still very much like a modernist's version of heaven. Minimal, with silvery steel vigas that shimmer in the ambient light, the interior of the house invites contemplation of the art installed on the walls and floor and displayed on shelves. But that is a pleasure reserved for those who are staring straight in front of them. Once they pivot to the right, the view is all that matters, exhilarating but also calming. "It's the blue sky here," says the husband, perhaps thinking of Belgium where rainfall averages 200 days a year. His wife elaborates: "The sky here is 50 percent of our vision. It keeps me cheerful and optimistic."

Light

PRECEDING PAGES: Contemporary artworks in the principal bedroom include Susan York's *Diptych no. 1* and Constance DeJong's *Column II*, both explorations of precise geometrical form typical of the clients' collection as a whole.

OPPOSITE AND BELOW: A corridor links the principal bedroom to the dining room and to the hall beyond. The reflective surface of Gloria Graham's *Carbon of Carbon Dioxide* shimmers on the dining room wall. RIGHT: Theaster Gates's *Civil Tapestries II*, composed of decommissioned fire hoses and wood, hangs next to the fireplace and above *Cleave*, a cast-iron sculpture by Tom Joyce.

The expansive living area unfolds toward a wall of French doors that open into the landscape. Clerestory windows just below the ceiling keep the space filled with natural light. Above the doors is Nic Nicosia's *M+M 35.5 Minutes*, a graphite circle drawn directly on the wall by the artist. Kate Shepherd's *Aaltohangman2.s6* hangs between the bookcases.

ABOVE: On the fireplace is a pre-Columbian granulite hatcha, or mace, from Ecuador. *Biomorphic*, an assemblage of white earthenware forms by Yuichiro Komatsu, is displayed on the coffee table. The hand-forged fireplace screen is by blacksmith Caleb Kullman. OPPOSITE: A niche above the bed in the principal bedroom holds mementos that reflect the couple's travels and collecting over time.

The back courtyard that extends from the living area is enclosed on three sides and has the intimate appeal of a *hortus conclusus*. A crabapple tree blossoms extravagantly in the spring, a cloud of pink that offsets the minimal interior spaces. In the center is Antony Gormley's cast-iron sculpture *Guard*.

Sight

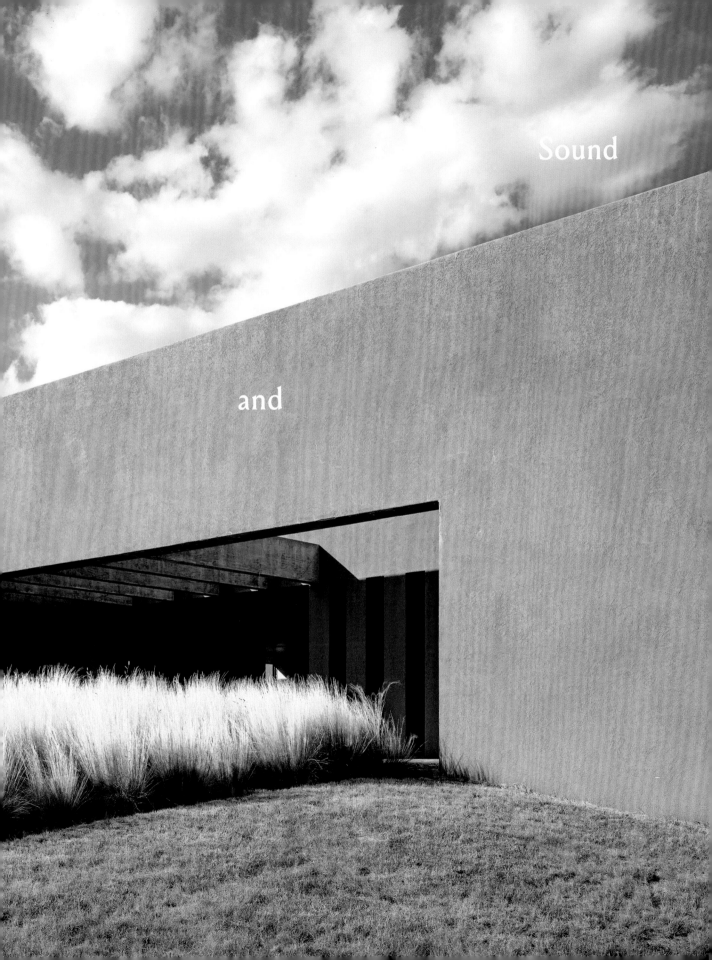

Sound

and

"I just wanted to wake up to sky and light and breathe fresh air," says Charles Churchward, who moved permanently to Santa Fe in the spring of 2012 after living in New York for forty years. There, Churchward was an art director for numerous publications including *Vanity Fair* and *Vogue*. The view from his full-floor urban loft was of the neighbor on the corresponding floor in the building across the concrete canyon—a nearly universal phenomenon in the congested city. But when the art director stationed his exercise bike in front of the open window and coincidentally saw a cartoon in *The New Yorker* magazine depicting the silhouette of a man on an Exercycle as viewed through the neighbor's window, the urban dweller decided it was time to leave the city.

The New Jersey native had been living part-time in Santa Fe for fifteen years, and he knew he didn't want to buy a house influenced by the city's popular pueblo-style architecture. He was also aware of the dearth of postwar dwellings. One rainy day his realtor drove him down a muddy road to see a modernist house built by Ralph Ridgeway, a local architect and builder who had once worked for Frank Gehry in Los Angeles, as his own residence. Sited on a ridge in the foothills of the Sangre de Cristo Mountains, the single-story building showed the influence of brutalism with its blocky geometric profile and cement composite facade. Glass doors and walls are transparent interruptions in the monolithic form, and a walk-through with the realtor quickly revealed that light also streamed in via skylights that extend along one side of every room. Wood beams on the living room ceiling alluded to vigas of traditional Santa Fe construction, but in this house, the sunlight playing against them created graphic shadows, which designer Churchward felt right at home with. The same dynamic occurs as the sunlight strikes the beams over the patio outside the living room and dining room.

Churchward purchased the sophisticated house, which had elements that reminded him of his spacious New York loft space, only better. "Suddenly I had walls where I could hang all my art," he explains. And he had rooms—a long entry, the living room and a library on the left, dining room and kitchen in the middle, and two wings on the right, each with its own bedroom suite.

Every room is dominated by the views, which Ridgeway calibrated with a compass so that they are revealed to best advantage through floor-to-ceiling windows or sliding glass doors. "I hate hallways," says the architect, "so every room in the house was set up to see a view as you walk in." Ridgeway's exacting measurements are appreciated by the art director whose career was defined by the ability to judge the visual impact of a magazine spread—smaller than the views of the desert horizons but similar ideologically as a way to frame a visual concept.

Churchward made a few changes to the house, brightening the interior brown Rastra walls (insulated concrete forms) to white and revising the landscape. The house is south of Santa Fe, in an ecosystem that reflects its place below the mythical snow line (which is also Interstate Highway 25). Weather here is more temperate than in the city or the nearby mountains. Churchward celebrated the more open terrain by planting rows of feather reed grass at the entry and behind the house. "I like to watch the wind whip the grass around," he says. Pleasures in this part of the world are multisensory, and Churchward relishes them all—even the swelling wail of coyotes that crescendos into ecstatic yipping before dropping off into deathly quiet. Some humans find the sounds spooky, but not Churchward, who is now a connoisseur of the predators' crazed chorus that cuts through the midnight silence, synergistic and frenzied. "I wanted sound around me that I didn't create," he says.

A bed of undulating Mexican feather grasses animates the landscape in front of the patio at the back of the house. The portal is paved with a red and light-gray Bisazza chevron cement tile.

OPPOSITE: The east wall is pierced by tall, narrow windows that complement that pattern of light from the skylights above the vigas. ABOVE: *Untitled, 1960* by Churchward's mentor, Alexander Liberman, hangs outside the dining area. OVERLEAF: Pop artist Peter Dayton's painting of pink tulips is the focal point of the living room, where black-leather Lc2 chairs define one seating area and a B&B Italia sofa defines another, with red Tato footrest between them. The black-and-white chaise is from Capellini.

OPPOSITE: An Eileen Gray Bibendum chair sits below a Sidney Geist wood wall sculpture from 1942. Indian Kokomo Gold sandstone floor tiles throughout the living spaces are original to the house. ABOVE: In the library, *Omega XIII, 1959* by Alexander Liberman fills a wall. A Charles Pollock chair for Knoll is paired with a Marc Newson Embryo chair.

BELOW: In the principal bedroom Eileen Gray side tables flank the Cassina bed, which is backed by twentieth-century French Plexiglass folding screens behind the headboard. A Pierre Paulin Ribbon chair and footstool offer a comfortable spot for reading. OPPOSITE: The path to the house is paved with crushed granite, the color a complement to the terra-cotta stucco walls. A fully glazed entrance and tall openings in the far wall allow a view through from the entry to the patio and the Sandia Mountains beyond.

Mad About Saffron

Stephen Beili

The quality of light in Santa Fe is much praised for its clarity and abundance. When it arrives in the mornings, there is nothing coy about it—the light materializes as if in full dress, illuminating the waking world with even-handedness. Six brilliant yellow panels are like sunbeams incorporated in Lori Lanier's front gate and demonstrate how a functional element can project a message about the good nature of a house, its owner, and its designer Stephen Beili.

"Yellow is the first color our eyes register as we approach the house," says Beili. There were also practical reasons for using the yellow recycled resin in the rusted steel slatted gate. The narrow end of Lanier's wedge-shaped, sharply sloping site is street-side. "We knew we'd have to put the garage in the front and the house in back of it, but we did everything we could to take attention away from that," he explains. The gate is eight steps down from the street; the front door to the two-story house is eight steps farther, halfway down the rugged lot. It's a colorful journey to the front door passing through a chartreuse-walled courtyard that runs the width of the house. The shady space is sliced lengthwise by a rill fed by water recirculating out of a rusted steel panel. It's punctuated with twenty-eight brightly colored chartreuse, pink, and yellow dots, the tip ends of acrylic rods that Lanier, a realtor, found in a plastics supply store in Albuquerque. At the other end of this little paradise is a seating area in front of a brilliantly orange fireplace. There, Lanier and her partner, Lee Klopfer, a photographer and landscape architect, can take a break from working in their "yard." The courtyard is the only place on the craggy lot that offers horticultural opportunity, which the couple has made the most of.

A red door signals that this is the way inside the compact house overlooking the city's East Side and the Sangre de Cristo Mountains. Despite the illusion of symmetry, the high-ceilinged room slyly breaks the rules: "It doesn't have four corners," notes Beili, who used glass sliding doors on the left for access to the portal; on the right, a stairwell leading downstairs delivers a sense of height and depth to the room. Sleek vigas float overhead, but, with space between them and the ceiling, there is a palpable sense that the room has taken a deep breath. In between, the fireplace is off-center, pushed to the right to make room for the view.

Color, it turns out, was the source of a wellspring of appreciation for Santa Fe architectural style, which Beili admits he found unnerving when he moved to nearby Galisteo to join his parents in 1992. "I was in shock," says Beili, who had been working at the Los Angeles architecture and design firm Morphosis. "I didn't know a nicho from a viga. I stayed here for twelve years, and I was trying to leave the whole time." He did, in fact, leave, and went to Asheville, North Carolina.

Beili came back to Santa Fe in 2012, and "this time it felt perfect." In the meantime, he had studied the work of Ricardo Legorreta, a disciple of the Mexican architect Luis Barragán, who blended the building traditions of his native country and modernism. Legorreta's design paradigm includes geometric shapes, vivid colors, and plays of light and shadow. The Mexican architect designed several buildings in Santa Fe including a residence and the Zocalo Condominiums, where Beili had lived. "Legorreta's use of color helped me find my place here," says Beili. Lanier and Klopfer's residence is an exuberant celebration of the colors that flourish seasonally in this part of the country: the brilliant yellow of prickly pears, hot pink of cholla cactus blossoms, and the chartreuse sheen on the skin of crabapples that grow wild in Santa Fe. They are the colors that are the exception to the rule in this desert landscape. They signify spring, regeneration, and a hardy determination to flourish in a harsh environment—and they make Lori Lanier, who loves color, happy.

135

OPPOSITE: Concrete terraced steps lead to a brilliant red front door;
a pocket garden the stretches across the front of the building.
ABOVE: A yellow bed on a wood platform is suspended from the
porch ceiling. The porch cantilevers over the rocky descent of
the hill, creating an overhang next to the principal bedroom below.

ABOVE: Designer Stephen Beili placed the fireplace off-center in the room—as well as off-center on the chimney—to maximize access to the floating portal and view beyond the sliding glass doors.
OPPOSITE: Plaster walls reflect light streaming in from the skylight embedded in the ceiling. The painting is by Kevin Tolman.

OPPOSITE: The window wall in the kitchen overlooks the seating and fireplace in the courtyard where meals are often served.
ABOVE: The principal bath downstairs is a world of its own, with a wall of windows offering a limitless view. The concrete trough sink extends the width of the room, with mirrors suspended mid-view; the tub is at hand, with its own window and breeze.

Yellow stucco walls and an orange fireplace extend the living space of this compact residence. The hearth wraps around the enclosure creating seating and a shelf to display plants—all enhanced by bubbling water coursing through the channel in the middle of the space. Facing the fireplace is a chartreuse wall on which the fountain—a perforated rusted steel panel—is mounted.

Perfectly

When a photographer and his wife, a stylist and producer, bought a rambling 1940s-era adobe house near the top end of Upper Canyon Road, there were tantalizing hints that the preceding owner had lived a life of gusto there. Paint splatters on the basement bedroom floor confirmed what the couple had heard—an artist lived in the quirky walled redoubt. Painted decoration—such as the two stylized black horses nose-to-nose on a kitchen window—corroborated that the cooking area was also a favorite spot. And then a neighbor walked by and asked if the pair could still hear laughter and the tinkle of glasses lingering in the house. "We thought the owner was a famous person from Hollywood," says the wife. She was partly right—the owner was famous locally, and lots of celebrities from Hollywood figured into her life.

New Orleans native Rosalea Murphy came to Santa Fe in the early 1940s. She never left, formally institutionalizing her partying personality into a restaurant in 1944. The Pink Adobe and its bar, The Dragon Room, became a destination and then a legend. Murphy held court there and in the house where the pair now live.

The two-story building, tucked sideways into a bend in the road, overlooks the city; the street side discreetly invites entry under an arch that anticipates a terraced garden to the left and a portal to the right. Sheltered by the portal, the front door opens onto a wide hall and living room; at the far end French doors in the dining area frame the city view and the mountains. To the right, are a breakfast nook and kitchen; to the left of the entry a hallway leads to the guest bedroom. Above it is the husband's media room. A lounge, to the left of the living room, connects to the principal suite.

All of the rooms had seen their best days by the time the couple arrived in 2018. Neglect and eccentric construction strategies meant that their renovation would be extensive. But the house had an ad hoc flair and lots of mystery—some interior walls, for instance, were inexplicably built right over other walls. The couple concluded that they had to accept the oddities; the construction itself was solid and details exquisitely achieved. Another conundrum: none of the floors were the same material—some were brick and others were flagstone (not all the same color, either). The free-spirited flooring scheme became obvious when the couple tore down walls to open up the living area. "It was impossible to remove those floors," says the wife.

Their solution was to commemorate the incompatible materials, marking the transition (or lack of it) between rooms with a narrow band of pebbles set in concrete, yet another texture in the unorthodox mix. As an improvisational gesture the pebbly strips capture the spirit of the house. They also are a reminder that in Santa Fe architecture tends to be more subjective than rigorous. That was a relief to the artistic couple: "We had been asked for perfection during our careers," says the wife. "We have moved away from that kind of self-torture. Our current mantra is Imperfection is Beauty."

Imperfect

PRECEDING PAGES: A serene corner of the bedroom combines a vintage Palazzetti lamp with a vintage leather chair and Saarinen table; behind them is a photograph from the homeowner's Insincere Landscapes series. The rya rug—depicting an aerial view of northern New Mexico—was woven by the homeowner when she was a teenager. ABOVE AND RIGHT: The lounge connects the living area to the principal bedroom. Above the sofa are photographs of China by one of the homeowners. The Team 7 Austria credenza opposite displays a collection of Asian objects. An abstract work by South Korean artist Il Lee hangs above. The carved wood lintel above the opening to the living area is original to the house.

A black-leather Knoll Salsa loveseat faces Water/Mountain coffee tables designed by the homeowner; the Mira Nakashima Conoid bench accentuates the sensuality of the stone floors; a "book landscape" by one of the homeowners stretches along the George Nakashima shelf. Above it, a photograph taken on Hong Kong's Victoria Peak in 1997.

ABOVE: A breakfast nook and banco seating with Oaxacan textiles in the kitchen are original to the house. The mesquite wood bench in the foreground is the owners' design. OPPOSITE: The owners designed and fabricated the dining tabletop, repurposing Chinese almanac pages inset by craftsman John Semrad in white oak. The custom leather and oak benches are by Team 7 Austria. The silhouette of the Moooi Random pendant is particularly striking against the sunset sky.

The kiva fireplace in the principal bedroom is original to the house. The Team 7 Austria bed seems to float on the seafoam-colored flokati rug, a reference to the aquatic theme throughout the house. Above is a DIY Coral Pendant by David Trubridge.

ABOVE: A kudu horn over the dining room fireplace belonged to the father of one of the homeowners. The Water chair references archaic Chinese characters; it is the companion to a Mountain chair elsewhere in the room. The Marc Riboud vintage photograph is from his China series. OPPOSITE: An adobe-framed Spanish colonial gate opens into the zaguan, a pathway linking the main house with the garden and portal. The terraced garden is planted with piñons, fruit trees, and evergreens mixed with ornamental trees and shrubs.

154

Out on a Ledge

The Sangre de Cristo Mountains northeast of Santa Fe are about fifteen miles away from Jim Rimelspach and David Arment's home in the foothills. Even at 6,000 feet below the peaks, the foothills are steep, and some of the edges recede precipitously, not yielding much space for a house. But the couple's stacked stone, stucco, and glass residence is long and lean, slipped below grade into the hillside so that just its profile and the front door are visible from the street. The house discreetly aligns with the surrounding rocky terrain, and, with plantings such as aspens, piñons, and blue spruce, the building seems comfortably ensconced on its selvadge of a sloping fold in the topography. "This house feels like we are in the wild," says Rimelspach, who notes that it's not unusual to see a bear walking across the driveway or a bobcat who regularly lounges on the portal, basking in the sunset's glow.

The couple has been living in Santa Fe since 2000, but they were in town frequently in the early 1990s when Rimelspach, design director for Dallas-based architecture firm Wilson Associates, was working on the Inn of the Anasazi. Rimelspach also oversaw the hotel renovation in 2006. Arment, an art consultant, worked on the Oprah Winfrey Leadership Academy for Girls in Gauteng Province, South Africa. It was there that Arment discovered his calling. "I said, 'Wouldn't it be great if we found contemporary craft for the school?'" It was a way to connect with South African artists and artisans, and in the process, Arment fell in love with Zulu baskets locally fashioned out of recycled telephone wire. At the time, the baskets weren't considered exceptional, but Arment has amassed one of the world's most comprehensive collections of the joyfully colorful containers that were once dismissed as tourist souvenirs.

Art and travel have always been the bond between the couple's professional and personal lives. The Rimelspach-designed house is now the setting for most of Arment's collection, a vivid selection of which is concealed on a wide wall of bookshelves behind sliding doors in the living area. The feeling that beyond the house's front door is a world full of beauty—both natural and man-made—is confirmed as soon as a guest descends the steps to the living area. To the left are an office and guest suite; to the right are a study and the principal suite. A kitchen and a living/dining area occupy the center of the house. Here, the wide-open, all-glass back of the rectilinear house seems to emerge from the rugged ridge, a material contrast to the inscrutable front facade. Beyond and visible through the wall of sliding glass doors, is a vaulting view of the Sangre de Cristo Mountains, which glow pink or red at sunset.

There are ways—architectural as well as practical—that the Rimelspach/Arment residence is similar to the cliff dwellings of the ancient people who lived in this part of New Mexico in the early centuries of the previous millennium. Sleek and efficient, their dwellings were tucked into or under the edges of cliffs, offering both prospect and refuge. Relying on a way to see out and to feel protected at the same time is just as rewarding now as it was in the thirteenth century. It confers a sense of rightness about the environment that extends beyond geographical boundaries. "One of the things we love about Africa," says Rimelspach, "is that we feel like we are in a natural world where things are the way they are supposed to be. That's how we feel about living here, too."

PRECEDING PAGES: A slab of local rock supports a steel I-beam to create the entry portal, a dramatic juxtaposition of rough and industrial. At the base of the birch trees Jeremy Thomas's inflated steel sculpture provides a contrast. ABOVE: *Melrose* by Mark Sheinkman dominates the study. Ashanti stools are on display on a shelf by the window, with traditional Zulu black clay beer pots on the table. OPPOSITE: Massive wood columns made from trees salvaged from the 2013 Pecos Canyon fire line the window wall in the living room. Floors are polished concrete, and walls are natural plaster, below bleached ceiling beams. A Juan Hamilton sculpture occupies the niche next to the fireplace. The painting above is by Juan Uslé.

Arment's collection of Zulu telephone-wire baskets is
displayed near the dining table designed Rimelspach. An
acrylic burnished on bleached-linen painting entitled
Sand Bend Draw by Johnnie Winona Ross hangs over the
console. Below are sculptures by Carol Sue Ross and Bruno
Romeo and a photograph of an owl by Masao Yamamoto.

161

ABOVE: Frank Gehry's Cross Check chair is placed in the bedroom below a John McCracken wall sculpture and next to shelves where Ashanti stools from Ghana, vintage Navajo rugs and blankets and kachina dolls reside. OPPOSITE: Arment and Rimelspach have a significant collection of late nineteenth- and early twentieth-century Acoma *ollas*, or water jars, displayed on shelves in the living room.

In the principal bedroom, the geometry of the recessed fireplace and deep shelves contrasts with the open view of the landscape. A Navajo rug on the bed is a strong graphic statement; next to the window a Saarinen Womb chair is a favorite reading spot. The painting is by Juan Uslé.

Into

the

Santa Fe is surrounded by the Santa Fe National Forest—2,435 square miles of piñons, firs, aspens, meadows of rustling grasses, and a quiescent volcano with a 15-mile-wide crater. Mountains rise to more than 13,000 feet. Lush and dense, the forest is a recreational destination, but it is mysterious, too, with trails that lead away from civilization. The ancient Puebloans flourished here from the mid-twelfth to the mid-seventeenth centuries. Bandelier National Monument has the mute self-possession of a secret world now forsaken. The counterpoint between outdoor adventurers and ancient civilizations makes this enigmatic part of the world appealing to people who enjoy complexity as well as privacy.

Jack Woody's compound is at the end of a road that terminates at the forest. The art book publisher, owner of Twelvetrees Press and Twin Palms Publishers, bought the six-acre property and a tiny adobe house in 1988 from a skeet-shooting Texan who lived there in seclusion. The location suited Woody, too, but he needed more space for his book collection. Woody consulted with Santa Fe-based architects Antonio Pares and Laura Van Amburgh for a solution. "I always have to have a library, wherever I live," he explains.

An adjacent hillside blocked horizontal expansion, so Woody built a two-story addition above and around the original house. The new construction extends the box-like structure with a dining room, kitchen, guest room, and a spacious living room with French doors

that open into a private front courtyard. The principal suite is upstairs. The original living room is now the publisher's library.

The Woody compound is hidden from the road by stacked stone and stucco walls and secured by a rusted steel-panel gate. When the gate is wide open, a sunny gravel courtyard spreads into view, flanked on the left by Woody's glass-walled office with a guest suite wrapped behind. On the right, a garage is a de facto book warehouse. Two ponds establish the boundary between public and private, and Woody's house stands in the shadows beyond. The three buildings are precisely modern, as if etched into the bristling and willful landscape.

Woody designed his gardens to be understated, anchored by an eccentrically pruned Russian olive tree. But, behind the house, native grasses and wildflowers grow amok, a messy boundary that gradually dissolves into the sumptuous forest. At Woody's house, the unknown is never underestimated—bears, bobcats, and an occasional mountain lion wander up to drink out of the two ponds, a reminder of natural priority that the reclusive editor likes. As the publisher of exquisitely produced books of photographic and gay history, Woody has explored the discord between safety and the fearsome throughout his career. Its misalignment is a fascinating phenomenon he celebrates both professionally and at home.

Van Amburgh+Pares+Co.

Wild

PRECEDING PAGES: The lanky branches of a Russian olive tree are a minimalist screen in front of Woody's office, a separate building that defines one side of the entry courtyard. ABOVE: Scored concrete floors and exposed wood framing the door in Woody's studio are a spare setting for the publisher's diverse collections. A Gustav Stickley chair is pulled up to an Aalto table. OPPOSITE: The profile of the staircase becomes a decorative feature of the entryway with the pattern of the steps outlined in stucco against the plywood walls for a *tansu* effect. In front, a chair attributed to Richard Neutra reflects Woody's appreciation of Japanese style.

Hand-troweled pale-green plaster walls create an atmospheric mystique in the living room, a subtly emotive backdrop for furniture Woody has collected. He discovered the yellow silk sofa in a resale shop on La Brea Avenue in Los Angeles; the purple lounge chair is a find from the local Goodwill. A low table by T. H. Robsjohn-Gibbings for Widdicomb displays a tall Russel Wright vase. On the mantel is a nineteenth-century Japanese tool for tamping mud floors.

Into the Wild

Double doors in the office face the front door across a pond in the courtyard. To the side is the guest house with a white Architectural Pottery vase from the 1950s on a pink base in front of the entry.

ABOVE: Now in the center of the house, Woody's library—where he keeps rare first editions and favorite books from other publishers—was the living room of the original adobe building. The Saltillo tile is original, as is the fireplace. A Chinese abacus serves as a fire screen. OPPOSITE: Woody's grandmother, Helen Twelvetrees, was a 1930s-era Hollywood star; the framed poster promotes one of her movies.

The desert and its contradictions have figured prominently in Bonnie Lynch's life and art. The ceramic sculptor grew up on a ranch outside El Paso in the Chihuahuan Desert—visibility is seventy miles there, and the distant views of the Guadalupe Mountains invite an appreciation of the maximalism of the desert space and the integral minuteness of its composition. "I was outside most of the time when I was growing up," says Lynch, "literally close to the rocks and stones in this rugged terrain." Occasionally, tiny flowers would bloom after a rain, or a bug that hadn't made an appearance in years would sally forth, launching its way across a landscape that is mostly brown, beige, and gray. The effect on the artist's own palette, as well as on the materiality of her smoke-fired vessels, was decisive. "You have to look closely to see what's beautiful, and that gave me a strong preference for minimalism."

Lynch's house is the soul of minimalism. The stucco, glass, and steel structure is spare, leaving the impression that it's composed of a few walls supporting a horizontal plane. Because the roof is flat we can assume it's there, but it seems as if the exterior walls stand with the dignity of columns you might stumble across in a modernist ruin. Inside, floor-to-ceiling windows are expansive slices of see-through space that free the living/dining area, Lynch's office, and her bedroom from the heavy constraints that walls impose on a room. The L-shape formed by the conjunction of public and private wings partially frames a courtyard, which is the view from every room, except the guest wing. The guest suite is connected to the house by another glass-walled courtyard, which is visible from the entry procession to the front door, as well as from the main courtyard. There are no secrets in this house, where the dynamic of solidity and transparency revitalizes the interplay between hard and soft, matte and glittering, unseen and seen.

The contrapuntal relationship of opposing forces also informs the ceramist's work—her coil-built, hand-built vessels look as fragile as if they were spun from sugar, but they are defiantly sturdy. "It would take a hammer to destroy one," says Lynch, whose pieces have been acquired by the Judd Foundation and the Menil Collection in Houston. The vessels are saggar-fired, a process first used by the Chinese to keep wood ash from the wood-burning kiln from falling onto their celadon glazed pottery. Today, the combustible material is inside the saggar (a box placed inside the kiln) and that's what colors the surface of the pot. The results are always a surprise, which Lynch loves. Her pieces range in size from elegantly curved, flattened forms with uneven edged rims that are small enough to hold in the palm of your hand to spherical shapes suited to setting on the floor to sculpture-like ovoid pieces that are as tall as a person. All demand a close look—like the desert, the elements that appeal are minuscule and their colors (blue, brown, gray, black) ethereal. In her house, the vessels add sensuality to the otherwise spare spaces, their textural subtlety a prologue to the desert view outside.

PRECEDING PAGES: The entry is set into the side wall of the main building, which contains the living area, Lynch's office, and her bedroom. The garage to the left is connected to the house by a glazed hallway. ABOVE: *Quarry VII*, a drawing by Lynch's sister Linda Lynch, hangs over an antique Chinese console. *The Ledger of Attachments*, made of compressed antique Japanese ledger paper by Gail Rieke, reflects the sinuous shapes in Lynch's work. OPPOSITE: Glass beads woven at a women's cooperative in Zimbabwe hang on the office wall. One of her vessels sits next to the window; a stack of Ethiopian trays makes a sculptural impact.

OPPOSITE: *Quarry II* by Linda Lynch hangs in the dining room above one of Bonnie's vessels. The live-edge walnut dining table is by Sam Takeuchi. ABOVE: In the office, one of Lynch's shell vessels sits between *Distant Line* by Debra Salopek and a photograph by Kate Breakey. OVERLEAF: The rich brown of the ipe floors shows off two vintage velvet sofas; the chairs are Hungarian from the 1930s. A vessel by the legendary Japanese ceramist Tsujimura Shiro sits on a keyaki wood coffee table by Takeuchi.

BELOW: The minimalist dining area includes only a table by Sam Takeuchi and a pair of antique Chinese chairs.
OPPOSITE: Lynch blends vintage and rustic in her bedroom. A pink satin settee that belonged to her mother is juxtaposed with an antique Senufo bed from West Africa used as a bench at the foot of the bed.

A Wall Runs Through It

A Corten building linking two concrete walls marks the entry to a courtyard and the way into the house. The approach is deliberately compressed so that when the house opens up at the back, the effect is dramatic, focusing on the view and Elliot Norquist's *Red Sculpture*.

"The beauty of working in New Mexico," says David Lake, principal in Lake | Flato Architects, "is that you have to think about the sanctity of the wall." Historically, the wall is the most conspicuous building strategy in this desert landscape. As a barrier, it is a defense against a capricious climate, rowdy terrain, and predators. But, as an extension of a building, it offers a way to safely outstretch a living space into a severe environment. "Walls embody the spirit of architecture here," Lake says.

This crisply avant-garde Corten and stucco house is an exploration of walls—an appreciation of the wall as enclosure, as a way to frame a view, as a signifier of texture and color. "In modernist design," the architect notes, "solid walls are often replaced with glass." But this contemporary interpretation of a hacienda—grounded by three solid rectangular volumes framed by rusted corrugated steel facades—departs from modernist motifs. Lake and his art-loving client rejected default modernist gestures such as vast expanses of glazing, despite a spectacular view to the Sangre de Cristo Mountains. Instead, to protect the owner's collection of photographs, prints, paintings, and video works, Lake devised alternate pathways to fill the house with light. He placed walls where windows would have seemed the obvious recourse. They frame the views but subvert direct light—its presence is felt but never confronted.

Muscular stucco walls extend into the land, warding off the terrain and establishing a series of courtyards between the garage and the main living wing. The two flanking walls are spanned by a bridge that is both the upper part of a portal shielding an entry court as well as a space for staff quarters. Inside the main house, an entry ramp is lit by clerestory windows above panels where the rotating collection is displayed. Space seems compressed in the sloping gallery (designed that way for accessibility) before it terminates two feet lower at a luminous living area. Like a tube of light, the room is completed at each end with glass walls—open to the views but protected by deep overhangs that intervene between direct sunlight and the interior space.

The room is the center of life in the house—the kitchen at the east end is embraced by a high-roofed portal; to the west is a generous seating area, best when the Sangre de Cristo mountain range takes on the prismatic blush of the setting sun. Windows are few and far between in this singular realm, less than 25 percent of the wall area of the entire house. But they are judiciously placed. A window behind the dining table reaches up five feet from floor level, a frame through which to view one of the verdant courtyards during meals. The windows offer a periodic revelation of an undomesticated outside world from the vantage point of a quiet interior. "The owner liked to feel immersed in the wild," says Lake.

Across the room, another window overlooks the entry courtyard punctuated by a collection of five-hundred-year-old Japanese snow lanterns—crafted from stone, bronze, and sometimes iron, they were originally used in Buddhist temples to line and illuminate a path. Now they indicate another path, where intense works of art—such as the oversized Richard Avedon portraits, part of the series In the American West, still have shock value, perhaps even more so out of a sterile museum setting. "My client was irreverent," says Lake. "And a free spirit—to be an art collector you can't be conventional."

ABOVE: A high ceiling and overscaled windows make the kitchen seem grand as does the 1957 Erik Höglund chandelier. The roof extends over the outdoor dining space, supported by slender metal pipe that does not interfere with the view. Ceramic teapots from the owner's collection are displayed on the island. OPPOSITE: Richard Avedon photographs line a wall in the living space, beckoning visitors through the dimly lit entry passage.

Full-height window walls at both ends of the living area and clerestory windows between the ceiling and walls fill the space with diffused natural light.
A vintage Navajo rug is a companion to the Richard Avedon photograph of a Texas rattlesnake skinner from the In the American West series. Above the sofa, an orderly grid of Ed Ruscha's parking lot photographs contrasts with the rugged terrain outside.

A Wall Runs Through It

The house is built around interior courtyards planted with grasses and aspens. The entrance is unassuming, marked by steps down to sandstone rock and slab terrace. Beyond the walls of the courtyards, the landscape reverts to its natural state, viewed up close from pathways that wind through the piñon forest.

A Wall Runs Through It

OPPOSITE: The corridor leading to the living area is also a gallery, dramatically illuminated with LED lighting in rotating colors. John Baldessari's *Agave Plant, R,O,Y,W,G,B,V (with Black Post)* is installed at the end. ABOVE: Even the natatorium becomes an art gallery—at the end of the lap pool is Kiki Seror's wall sculpture *Not of Her Body, Her Thoughts Can Kill, Dulcinea*. Aquatic-themed works on the walls include contemporary photographs by Muzi Quawson, Miklos Gaal, Karine Laval, and Mads Lynnerrup.

196

Built

to

Fit

The three-story, earthy green- and sage-colored stucco house where James David and Gary Peese live has a bird's-eye view of the burning of Zozobra at Fort Marcy Park down the hill. The ritual incineration of the fifty-foot-tall, paper-stuffed marionette has occurred every September since 1926 (public gathering for the burning was banned in 2020 because of the pandemic). Part ghost, part monster, Zozobra is considered the embodiment of gloom; celebrants write their woes on paper and dispatch them into the flames. The tripartite hillside house offers ringside seating for this yearly spectacle; at other times, the view of the Jemez Mountains in the distance is a calmer prospect, stoic by day but aglitter at night with the lights of Los Alamos forty miles away. Only after David and Peese bought their property did the pair realize that neither view was guaranteed—the neighborhood on the outskirts of downtown has no height or density restrictions. When the lot next door came on the market in 2009, David and Peese bought it that afternoon.

There was personal history embedded in the two existing ramshackle structures on the site. Set apart and at right angles, the one on the left was a small concrete-block casita, a rectangular companion to the 900-square-foot adobe house, hand-built on weekends in the 1970s by the owner's son-in-law. David and Peese hired Santa Fe architect Gabriel Brown, principal in Praxis Design Build, to renovate the casita while they continued to run their landscape design firm in Austin. That was in 2010. After they sold the business, the pair decided to use the casita as a guesthouse and renovate the little handmade house. "All we need to do is add a bedroom," said David.

And a second floor. And thus they resumed what became a ten-year, three-phase construction process that inadvertently mimicked local custom. "It's a tradition here when annexing on to pueblo-style houses," says Brown. "You add a room when you have another child." The result is that houses expand organically, according to need and utility. "It grows out of the folk traditions of pueblos and dates back to the Anasazi," he says.

As traditional as the couple's aspirations were, their goal was all modern. The entry remained where it always was, but Brown expanded the foyer into the dining room to make room for a pantry on the right and a stairwell on the left. The kitchen remained the same size—an efficient arena for both, who love to cook; the living room became the dining room, the bedroom an office. And the 900-square-foot house grew to 1,600 square feet.

To keep proportions in scale, Brown made use of the descending grade of the lot, placing the two-story addition on the slope to make it look more compatible with the other two volumes of the house. The one on the left contains the original house; the one in the middle serves as the entry, set discreetly sideways from the street. Its oblique position is typical of pueblo-style architecture, oblivious to classically based Western architecture's love affair with statement-making facades. The volume on the right contains the new living room and principal suite upstairs and an office and garage downstairs, confirming the multi-dimensionality typical of the pueblo style. Plenty of space outside accommodates their extensive and elaborate gardens. Holistic and wholesome, this indigenous architecture found new value in the twentieth century.

The house is rich in provenance. David and Peese kept the longleaf pine floors, the viga ceilings, and the exterior walls. They also know who has lived in the unassuming dwelling—a well-known ceramist was first. Then her sister in Denmark inherited it, and David and Peese purchased the house from her. Gabe Brown also knew the family. And everyone knows that Rob Richardson built the house for his mother-in-law. It's a history that values beginnings; James David and Gary Peese joined in the process, linking their biographies to those who preceded them. "The kernel of the original house is still there," says Brown, acknowledging the indelibility of history in a place where everything ends up being connected.

PRECEDING PAGES: The rolled steel "origami" staircase, made by local metal fabricator Gabe Rippel, is located where the original entry was; it leads up to the addition that includes the principal bedroom. ABOVE AND OPPOSITE: The living room, built during the second phase of remodeling, is furnished with pieces brought from Austin, including a pair of Swedish leather sofas, an Oushak carpet, and the long wood table in front of the window. The steel fireplace is by architect Gabriel Brown.

OPPOSITE: The compact casita is now luxurious, with plaster walls and steel details on the freestanding fireplace and shelving; the ceiling and beams are original as are the floors.
ABOVE: The principal bedroom is also well articulated, designed to accommodate pieces from David and Peese's previous home; the Michael Tracy painting above the bed is a precise fit.

OPPOSITE: The kitchen is the same size and shape as the original, with its ponderosa pine ceiling and vigas now sandblasted for a more contemporary feel. David and Peese added the island and the pegboard (a tribute to Julia Child) for pan storage. ABOVE: Wooden container pots sit on a nineteenth-century Japanese chest.

OPPOSITE: A brick-paved dining area is located between the kitchen and an outdoor kitchen; orange Swedish rubber chairs surround the unfinished mahogany dining table, a handy place for Peese to set aside some of his prize tomato crop.
ABOVE: On the other side of the kitchen, a portal covers what was once the entrance to the original house, with a view to the casita.

Elements of Style

The panorama from Taryn Slawson's porch is like nothing else on earth. Both soft and harsh, the pink-tinged desert is encircled by distant plateaus. The vista is grandly stark and not immediately recognizable for what it is—a forty-mile-wide depression, one of three large basins that are part of the Rio Grande Rift. This rift—or linear zone whose crust is being slowly torn apart—is a 25-million-year-old scar that emerges at Leadville, Colorado, and comes to a stop in Chihuahua, Mexico. Santa Fe is right in the middle of it. From Slawson's lookout this desert seems less forbidding than it seems wonderful, the bottom fourth of a view that is mostly clouds and sky. In the radiant silence, sensory stimuli fade away, and all that remains is a feeling of well-being.

That was why Daryl Stanton built the modest house now owned by Slawson on this spot. "I've always been interested in anything that contributes to health," she says. "Part of my vision for a small contemporary house is that it is healthy." The adobe cube-like structure is both small—900 square feet—and healthy. Stanton installed formaldehyde-free cabinets and building plywood and used VOC-free paints throughout. The floors are concrete, and all lights are LED. And, with two walls of glass sliding doors in the living area, the cross-ventilation is robust.

Stanton's focus on well-being arose from a demonstration of her own vulnerability. In the late 1970s she became ill after a renovation of her West Hollywood home, when chemicals typical in building and decorating materials saturated her residence with toxins. That discovery was the beginning of a long career. Today, the entrepreneur is the owner and founder of Tansucasa, a Santa Fe-based company specializing in designing and building small dwellings that merge health, sustainability, and lifestyle. "My passion is simpler small houses," she says. "It's even better if they are in a community." The companion to this house, a 450-square-foot structure also designed as a prototype, is across the courtyard, and is where the builder's mother lived.

Stanton sold both houses in 2015 to Slawson, who had been living in an Airstream travel trailer. "The trailer was my introduction to small living," says Slawson, who is a weaver. "In order to weave, I need quiet and I need to be alone so that I can focus on what I am doing." She liked the expansive views of Stanton's house and also the unmediated presence of the natural world—and she even made changes such as removing the screens on the sliding doors in order to exaggerate the exposure. Now, birds fly through—in one side of the house and out the other—much to her delight. "It's very exposed here," she says. "And it feels close to the stars." But watching storms appeals the most—here, the dire weather phenomenon reaches far beyond human scale, and it's easy to understand why ancient mythologies ascribed their sky-splitting effects to divine beings, usually in a disturbing way. "The lightning storms are so close," says Slawson, "and so beautiful." They are a rather violent manifestation of natural demands important to the way the Colorado native has chosen to live. "This is not a soft place to be," she says. "It's unforgiving and it forces you to pay attention."

The small scale and remote location of the house are ideal for weaver Taryn Slawson. She often spreads her work against the rusted steel fence panels to be photographed.

OPPOSITE: Pattern is a language for Slawson. The house is furnished with her bold compositions, which resonate with the vivid orange and brown stripes in the vintage Florence Knoll sofa. ABOVE: Her studio is at one end of the living space, where she works, stores yarns, and displays projects.

ABOVE: A long stitched runner hangs next to the bed. The window offers a glimpse of the stucco and steel in the companion house and the landscaped courtyard between them. OPPOSITE: The two houses frame a view of the Sangre de Cristo Mountains. Slawson designed the exterior spaces and the planting, which includes Russian sage, a staple in New Mexico.

In the Abstract

Before Seth Anderson was an architect, he was an artist. The New Mexico native whiled away some of his time in high school classes doodling in a notebook, perfecting the looping line and all its tightly wound digressions. Eventually his talent matured into a fascination with the simple line, a reductive obsession that Anderson now translates into sculpture and on a larger scale, architecture. Line, in Anderson's world, is the armature for geometric shape, an idea that presented itself in high school in Albuquerque where the young artist entertained himself drawing house plans. The pursuit presaged his career in architecture.

Not surprising, then, that the architect lives with his wife, Kristen—a sales representative for the biopharmaceutical company Amgen—and their two sons in a house he designed. The polymath also built it, and designed the interiors, much of the art, and the landscape. Anderson admits that his sculpture now looks like houses. The converse is also true: The one-story stucco, steel, and glass structure is assertively sculptural, a box adjacent to a 26-foot-long wall that intersects with the building at a right angle. About midway in its length, the wall veers upward, seemingly propping the house in place. The lower end of the wall underscores a mighty view of the Sangre de Cristo Mountains.

The exterior of the house is bold; Anderson uses the stucco exterior plane as an absolute boundary between tangible and intangible. Inside, the architectural rigor is relieved by natural light that suffuses the 14-by-30-foot living space and bounces off the white plaster walls and fireplace. Douglas fir beams (Anderson hand-painted them) define the ceiling in a procession that enlivens the room with airy vigor. They anticipate the kitchen, a room with the boxy volume of an abstract painting. The view out the window is sliced in half by a nearby courtyard wall.

The living room's good feeling is intentional. When the floor-to-ceiling sliding glass doors are open to the terrace, the living space doubles. "The ability to live both indoors and outdoors in Santa Fe encourages me to live minimally," Anderson says. By eliminating decoration, he believes that his rooms have a chance to develop their personalities on their own, often in unexpected ways and over time. "There is a commonality in both my art and my houses," he says. "I am trying to capture an intangible element of feeling and presence that may also, in the end, be a surprise. In a sense it's an art project."

PRECEDING PAGES: The living room is a composition of volumes and horizontal lines, emphasized by outlines of the hand-painted vigas against the "whitest white" ceiling; a mid-nineteenth-century Bolivian poncho is a dark counterpoint.
RIGHT: A handwoven "rainforest" basket made by members of Panama's Wounaan tribe is the centerpiece on the custom wood dining table, flanked on one side by Hans Wegner Wishbone chairs and on the other by molded Bertoia Shell side chairs. A Mexican ribbed ceramic lidded pot sits on the inset console.

In the Abstract

OPPOSITE: Wood-grained ceramic tile extends from the living room onto the covered patio that extends the living space.
BELOW: A low stucco wall underscores a view of the Sangre de Cristo Mountains. The front door is recessed into the box-like volume containing the entry hall with a wide window looking back onto the gravel courtyard. A canale channels rainwater from the roof into a rock-lined drain below.

OPPOSITE: The patio is behind the low entry wall; the view
looking back is to the Jemez Mountains. ABOVE: Driade chairs
are grouped around a piece of solid stone from Mexico
in a private courtyard off the study.

ABOVE: French doors in the principal bedroom open onto the patio. The shelves display Murano glass bowl and Day of the Dead dolls. OPPOSITE: The bath and dressing room are a calm transition between the public and private areas of the house. Antique Mexican pine doors with original hinges and circular clasps lead into the bedroom.

Patterns   of

Light and Dark

The high desert is a powerful spectacle—earth and sky fit together along a vast ragged horizon. The adjacency is conjugal, as sympathetic as two pieces of a puzzle—and because of that, the desert is a place where people feel grounded. When an arts-loving couple asked Scott Specht to design a house for them, the Austin-based architect knew that the 360-degree view of the Sangre de Cristo Mountains would be a defining factor in how the modernist house would take shape. Added to the mix were the stringent requirements of the Santa Fe building codes. Rather than compromising the design, the restrictions felt liberating to Specht.

Height limitations mandated that that the building could be no more than fourteen feet above grade. Specht capitalized on the limitation, digging deep into the site so that the entry courtyard, long narrow water feature, as well as the entire house are below the hilltop. The procession from entry to the courtyard is a drop of three to six feet. It's a descent that journeys through a wide-open garden and a huge opening in the wall that frames the view before passing a glass front door that gazes onto the wondrous sight of the mountains. At that point the living room is level with the ground.

Two concrete walls—perpendicular to each other—run through the house; they organize the living space. Both extend out into the landscape, one defining the front courtyard, the other framing a side courtyard. The entry vestibule faces north, separated from the living area a few steps down by one of the concrete walls. "Then there is the blast of that view," says Specht about the wall-to-wall panorama beyond. Expanses of glass are deeply shaded by elements of the cantilevered roof that create porches around the perimeter of the building. To the left is the garage and the principal bedroom. To the right is a guest bedroom; a lower level is for the children's rooms.

The quiet decor doesn't compete with the art on the walls, the stunning view, or the innate drama that the architect incorporated into the project. A narrow skylight runs the entire 125-foot length of one of the walls, casting changing shadows of the ceiling beams on the rough concrete as the sun moves through the house during the day—hence the name "Sundial House," which Specht uses to refer to the project. Light is an active component of the house, which has been designed with an elemental relationship to the land. "It's like an earthwork," Specht explains, referring to construction that alters the contour of the land. The concrete, steel, and glass house quietly engages with its surroundings, its straightforward lines and simple volumes bringing clarity to the dusty randomness of the juniper- and piñon-studded terrain. "Sometimes," Scott Specht says, "it's hard to tell which part of the house is inside and which is outside."

PRECEDING PAGES: A modern interpretation of a buttress rendered in board-formed concrete straddles the front courtyard and frames a mountain view. BELOW: Two massive concrete walls organize the house; a narrow skylight bisects the space, running the entire length of one of the walls.

A perfectly balanced view of the convergence of man-made and wild. From the back patio, recessed into the body of the house, nature can be enjoyed while dining at a concrete dining table or reclining on the chaise.

OPPOSITE: Board-formed concrete walls frame the opening to the living room, where panoramic views of the Sangre de Cristo Mountains command attention. ABOVE: Timber beams in the living room, a modernist interpretation of vigas, cast shadows against the rugged concrete over the span of the day. The painting is by Svenja Deininger. OVERLEAF: The house is known as "Sundial," alluding to the shadows cast by the vigas that mark the sun's passage across the sky. The three paintings above the fireplace are by David Simpson.

233

Large expanses of glass throughout the house are deeply shaded by the roof which is cantilevered over porches that extend around the perimeter of the house, creating a corner outside dining area and a shady portal off the principal bedroom.

Acknowledgments

Santa Fe is used to being in the spotlight. It is inured to being adored, to being written about, to being a destination. For all its familiarity with public attention, you would think that doing a book about homes and their owners in this city would simply be a matter of making the obvious more obvious. But in fact, people who live in this desert refuge like their privacy, and in many cases are here to dwell quietly, in peace. Being obvious is not their thing.

For that reason, Casey Dunn and I are indebted to those who opened up their residences to us so that we could feature their eccentric, sleek, funky, and/or stunning dwellings in our book. And about half of them did so in the middle of a pandemic. We are especially indebted to them for believing that opening their homes (if only vicariously) would alleviate some of the mental exhaustion we all have endured.

It is these people we thank, for understanding that a home is more than a structure—it is a dynamic relationship with its owners (both current and former), its possessions, and its setting. *Santa Fe Modern* would not have been possible without the participation of Seth and Kristen Anderson, David Arment and Jim Rimelspach, Bonnie Lynch, Charles Churchward, James David and Gary Peese, Sally and Tom Dunning, Jeanne and Michael Klein, Lori Lanier and Lee Klopfer, Linda Lynch, Max Protetch and Irene Hofmann, Eddie Nunns, Lauren and Brad Hunt, Taryn Slawson, Daryl Stanton, Rick and Cindy Torcasso, Jack Woody, and last but not least, those homeowners who wish to remain anonymous.

I am also grateful to friends and acquaintances who directed me to houses and homeowners they knew would be perfect for this book. They were, of course, right: Jessie Otto Hite, Kumi Masumoto, Sam Takeuchi, Lesley Crews Dyer and Mike Dyer, Ann Marie Koshuta, Vicky MacCulloch, Susan Stella, Thomas Lehn and Jane Lackey, Dave Campbell, and Sebastian Bizzari and Jeff Holbrook.

Thanks especially to photographic assistant and stylist Mary Elkins and and assistants Allen Corralejo and Rowdy Winters, and to our families and extended family: Tommy, Beverly, and Avery Dunn, and Sarah Weinstein Dunn and Charles Lohrmann. We are particularly grateful to our editor Elizabeth White whose insightful guidance and enthusiastic support has resulted in a book that is the happy final third in our popular "Modern" trilogy. Special thanks to designer Caleb Bennett, whose elegant design offers us a way through which we can all experience how thrilling it is to live in a spectacular setting that never allows an observer to take it for granted.

Library of Congress Control Number 2021935232

ISBN 978-158093-561-6

Design: Caleb Bennett

Printed in China

The Monacelli Press
65 Bleecker Street
New York, New York 10012